William Playfair

A General View of the Actual Force and Resources of France in January, M.DCC.XCIII

William Playfair

A General View of the Actual Force and Resources of France in January, M.DCC.XCIII

ISBN/EAN: 9783337780036

Printed in Europe, USA, Canada, Australia, Japan

Cover: Foto ©Suzi / pixelio.de

More available books at **www.hansebooks.com**

A GENERAL VIEW OF THE ACTUAL FORCE AND RESOURCES OF *FRANCE*, IN JANUARY, M.DCC.XCIII.

TO WHICH IS ADDED,

A TABLE, SHEWING THE DEPRECIATION OF ASSIGNATS, ARISING FROM THEIR INCREASE IN QUANTITY.

By WILLIAM PLAYFAIR.

Let not him that girdeth on his harnefs, boaft himfelf as he that putteth it off.

I KINGS XX. II.

SECOND EDITION.

LONDON:

PRINTED FOR JOHN STOCKDALE, PICCADILLY.

1793.

[Price One Shilling and Six-pence.]

A

GENERAL VIEW, &c.

AS a war has taken place between this country and France, it is of confiderable importance that the nation at large fhould be able to form, as near as poffible, a true idea of the force of their enemy.

The fituation of France is fuch as is quite new in the annals of the world; and the force of that wretched and divided people cannot be eftimated according to any common rules: hence it is, that, viewed in one way, that nation feems to have immenfe refources, and to be able, with impunity, to defy all Europe: viewed in other points, it is equally demonſtrable, that the internal factions of the country will ſoon reduce it to a ſtate of inſignificance.

We muſt not wonder then that opinions in this country are divided, and that the public newſpapers, which are ſo frequently the guides of public opinion with regard to the actual ſtate of affairs, as well as the records of recent facts, repreſent the ſtate of France, as to power and reſources, very differently, and each according to the favorite views of its conductors.

I claim the attention of the public for half an hour on this important ſubject, and without pretending to any perſonal merit as a politician or financier, I found my claim to attention on a fact; which is, that in May laſt I ſhewed the ſtate of French finances for the year 1792, in a much truer light than Mr. Cambon, deputy of the National Aſſembly, and now member of the Convention. His ſtatement and mine are both printed, and the facts are ſince in my favour: I aſſerted that eleven hundred French millions would be neceſſary for the year, and he eight hundred millions. The real ſum has been 1250 millions;

lions; but then I obſerved at the time, that I was under the mark, and he imagined he had gone beyond it; ſo that his error was very great, and mine inconſiderable.

As to affairs of general politics, I, in the ſame work (printed in Paris, and publiſhed in London) demonſtrated the impoſſibility of the conſtitution maintaining its ground, the ſettled tendency of the revolution to a civil war, and a ſort of republic, denouncing, at the ſame time, the ſchemes of the Jacobin emiſſaries upon England. I have had, and ſtill have, opportunities to know facts that very few Engliſhmen can know, and therefore attribute my being right intirely to this circumſtance; which, though it may not entitle me to exult on my penetration, gives me ſome right to claim attention from my countrymen.

We are told that France has 2,400,000 armed men ready to engage her enemies, when we ſhould be told that ſhe has 2,400,000 who are not able to keep peace in their reſpective departments.

We are told that France has diſcovered a method of being able to ſupport an expence of 7,000,000 ſterl. a month, when we ſhould be told that ſhe has found a method of running 7,000,000 a month in debt, without any poſſibility of ever paying it, and with a certainty of being very ſoon deprived even of that ruinous reſource.

We hear that France is free, and that the whole nation (a few Ariſtocrats excepted) is contented and happy; when there is neither ſafety for individuals, liberty of opinion, nor unanimity; the loweſt dregs of the people being in Paris, and every where elſe, the conductors and tyrants of thoſe who have the vanity to ſay they govern, and the weakneſs to imagine that any one believes them.

We are told by themſelves, that their ſucceſs in September, October, and November laſt, was owing to their courage and good generalſhip, when, in fact, it was owing to ill conduct, and great miſtakes in their enemies.

Let us throw aſide the veil which their republican gaſconade has thrown upon facts, and we ſhall ſoon ſee that France is only ſuperior to other nations in vanity, injuſtice, cruelty, and miſery; in theſe, we will allow, ſhe is ſuperior to the whole human race; but neither in freedom nor in force.

Firſt, then, there are more than two millions and a half of fighting men in France; for every man is armed, from the age of 16 to that of 60; and many I have ſeen bearing arms at 13 and at 70: there muſt, then, be more than the number ſpecified; there muſt at leaſt be four millions. This is an adroit manner, on their part, of telling a falſhood, and eſcaping cenſure: they under-rate the number to be thought within bounds; but then it is added, they *can ſend ſuch a number againſt their enemies*, which is very falſe.

Never was there a time when France could ſend fewer men into the field, for any continuance of time, and ſupply them with neceſſaries, than at preſent; becauſe, in all the towns and villages, they want guards againſt each other; becauſe there is no order, no regularity, and no induſtry among thoſe at home, to ſupply thoſe who are in the field: for this reaſon we have heard of ſo many complaints made to the National Aſſembly againſt the miniſter of war (Pache). The men had neither ſhoes nor breeches; for the 180 millions of aſſignats a month, could neither create taylors nor ſhoemakers. No, this enormous ſum, which, in the time of Auguſtus, would have paid the whole expences of the Roman empire for nearly half a year, by means of order and arrangement, could not clothe the armies of Dumourier and Cuſtine for one month.

Can there be a clearer proof than this of the neceſſity of order, arrangement, and induſtry, to create force; and can any thing ſhew more diſtinctly the fallacy of eſtimating revenue by reams of paper, or force, by the total number of armed men?

That the armed men may act, it is eſſentially neceſſary that there ſhould remain a ſtill greater number *unarmed*. The whole nation, "ſay they," is a camp; and preciſely, for that

that reaſon, there is not one regiment of well-accoutered ſoldiers.

The truth is, that it was by an exertion of the moſt violent nature, that numbers of men were collected ſufficient to oppoſe the duke of Brunſwick's army, which was but about 60,000 ſtrong. Whole villages were depopulated of the flower of their youth in the northern parts of France; and I ſay it from certain knowledge, that the numbers who died from diſeaſe and ſkirmiſhes, amounted, in three months, to three times the whole number of their enemies.

The whole frontier of France, the ſea-coaſt, and a few inacceſſible parts excepted, is become a ſort of theatre for the war; and I venture to predict, that when they are all covered in the manner that neceſſity will require, France will not be able to have, for any length of time, an army of 200,000 men in any one quarter; nor will that army ever be either well clothed or well fed.

So much for the force by land; ſo much for the millions that are to plant the tree of liberty at Vienna, Peterſburg, and Pekin; and to ſuch a number is actually reduced that army of breechleſs philoſophers, who are to fraternize all mankind, by ſpreading aſſignats and levying contributions.

With regard to their reſource in finances, that merits a very particular inveſtigation; for upon that, in a great meaſure, depends the length of time, during which the French nation will be able to tear herſelf to pieces, and to diſturb all Europe.

When the aſſignats were firſt iſſued, there was a great quantity of real ſpecie in France. The government created them rather for the payment of debts, than for the uſual purpoſes of the treaſury.

The lands of the clergy that were ſeized by the firſt aſſembly, ſerved as a pledge for the reimburſement, or rather annihilation, of theſe aſſignats; and there was thus a real value in the paper ſo created. The combination was by no means an ignorant nor fooliſh one; nor were precautions wanting to give that paper credit. Had the ori-

ginal

ginal ſyſtem been carried into execution as it was planned, and had it not been extended too far, and the aſſignats miſapplied, the ſcheme, great as it was, would have ſucceeded well, and might have had a happy termination.

To explain this, let us follow the aſſignats through their different ſtages; and, in ſpeaking of them, let us put all the ſums in ſterling money, to avoid confuſion; 24 livres being always counted equal to the pound ſterling.

The firſt creation of aſſignats, in the beginning of 1790, was but equal to about one-fourth of the currency in ſpecie which is reckoned to circulate uſually in the kingdom; and this ſum was, in great part, paid in the reimburſement of debts, contracted under different forms; ſo that, in the firſt inſtance, it went into the hands of perſons who were rich or eaſy.

As the church lands began to be ſold at the ſame time, and the aſſignats were taken at par in theſe purchaſes, though paſſing at a loſs in the common affairs of life *, the monied people ſo reimburſed were very likely to employ their aſſignats in purchaſing church lands, which, in fact, they did; and as all aſſignats paid for theſe lands were annulled and burned, the quantity of paper did not increaſe very faſt at firſt.

The progreſs of burning, and the hopes of peace, quietneſs, and a revenue from taxes, when the conſtitution ſhould be finiſhed, gave, deſervedly, conſiderable credit to a paper, which, ſince thoſe hopes have vaniſhed, and ſince its quantity has been ſo prodigiouſly increaſed, deſerves no credit at all; and, in fact, obtains not much. By degrees, however, the new aſſignats created became

* As there were no aſſignats for leſs than 200 livres, or about eight guineas, people were obliged to change them for ſilver or gold. The firſt day they appeared, they were changed at a loſs of three per cent. but that ſoon mounted to five, and by degrees, in about a year, to 10. The ſecond year they had got ſo far as 40 per cent. loſs againſt gold and ſilver, when a manœuvre re-eſtabliſhed them a little. They are, at preſent, only at 50 per cent. loſs. I ſhall hereafter ſhew why they are not lower, as they have not really any intrinſic value at this time.

more numerous, and ceasing to be paid to public creditors for reimbursements, began to be employed for every sort of payments, and supplied the place of taxes to the public treasury. The assignat paid to the poor, or to the merchant, ceased to be employed in a purchase of church lands; it was immediately passed in trade; the gold and silver, by degrees, became dear and scarce; small assignats became necessary, and were created; so that before the end of the year 1791, a traveller might go from one end of France to the other, and see neither gold, silver, copper, nor any currency but the assignats, which were at 28 per cent. loss.

The constitution was finished, and was accepted by that well-meaning, good-natured, and unfortunate king, who has so lately paid so dearly for his good intentions; who has expiated, in so cruel a manner, his fatal complaisance to a set of levellers, whose ambition and vanity could bear no superior; but who were too ignorant to see that they would themselves also be amongst the number of the victims which their own hands were preparing. Instead of tranquility and peace, the

the conſtitution brought on more troubles, and their termination ſeemed now not to be fixed. A general miſtruſt took place, mixt with deſpondency; and the aſſignats ſeverely felt the ſhock.

One hundred millions ſterling was ſuppoſed to be the amount of ſpecie circulating in France before the revolution; but when the louis-d'ors and crowns had entirely diſappeared, the quantity of aſſignats in circulation did not amount to more than 12 millions. This may be attributed to three cauſes: trade was at a ſtand, and therefore the maſs neceſſary for circulation was diminiſhed: 2dly. That portion of the money in the kingdom that was not in actual circulation, was in gold or ſilver; but whenever it was wanted for uſe, it was changed into aſſignats; for it is curious enough, that though at firſt, when people wanted to make ſmall payments, they bought ſilver with aſſignats: at laſt they bought aſſignats with ſilver, on purpoſe to pay away.

The third reaſon was, that the aſſignats went at par in the payment of debts, of rent, and for many other things, of which the price could not ſo ſoon be changed; and that people parted with their aſſignats very readily, and had no deſire to amaſs a kind of money that had neither intrinſic value; durability, nor even beauty to recommend it, by which means a ſmaller ſum, by circulating more quickly, replaced the gold and ſilver. That being once done, there was a new cauſe for the diminution of the aſſignats in value, and it is this cauſe which muſt ultimately deſtroy their value altogether.

Until that terrible 10th of Auguſt, (when I ſaw ſcenes of rage and horror, which I ſhall never forget) the ſame manner of creating aſſignats continued; that is to ſay, though the number was ſtill increaſing, yet they did not paſs the bounds of about two millions ſterling a month, and the whole maſs was then about 80 millions ſterling, (not counting thoſe that were burned); ſo that going on by the ſame progreſſion, it would yet have been 10 months before the original quantity of ſpecie would have been fully replaced by paper.

From

From this epoch we may, however, date the laſt progreſſion of exceſſive expence in the ſyſtem of paper. September alone coſt nearly eight millions ſterling; the ſubſequent months have each coſt nearly as much; ſo that, in fact, the creation of aſſignats, ſince Auguſt, is equal to above 32 millions ſterling; and in the ſpring, inſtead of diminiſhing, that expence muſt increaſe. The ſum now created is therefore about 112 millions ſterling of paper, and that is augmenting at the rate of ſix millions a month.

Add to this, that for ſome time paſt the neceſſity of manufacturing the aſſignats in great haſte, prevents all thoſe precautions which are neceſſary to avoid falſification. The wild acts of the Convention, ſurpaſſing even its predeceſſors in rage, delirium, and wickedneſs, and going, like a ſhip in a tempeſt, without any fixt guide, have deſtroyed that ſmall degree of confidence that had remained ſo long.

What, then, has preſerved any degree of credit to theſe aſſignats, ſeeing that there is no hope of reimburſement, but that, on the

contrary,

contrary, the quantity increaſes more rapidly than ever.

The cauſes are various: the firſt is, that the want of order and authority over the lower claſs of people, who, in fact, are the maſters, and who live chiefly on dry bread, has prevented the price of that article from being raiſed in any great degree; and it is a curious fact, that though all ſorts of luxuries have increaſed in price, the aſſignat loſes hardly any of its value againſt bread, or the buſhel of wheat, which ought naturally to have riſen along with ſilver. The aſſignat continues ſtill to pay debts, rent, and taxes, at par, which ſerves greatly to preſerve its value.

Another cauſe is, that in Paris, upon the Place de Victoire, where gold and ſilver uſed to be ſold, the ſellers have been, in a great meaſure, chaſed away ſince the 10th of Auguſt; and thoſe that have been left are employed by the treaſury, ſometimes, to bring a greater quantity of gold than is wanted, and, by fictitious bargains, influence the market. The courſe of exchange is, in a

great

great degree, regulated by the price of gold; and ever ſince Claviere has been in the department of finances, manœuvres of this kind * have been carried on to a great extent, and with conſiderable ſucceſs.

Although it is clear, that what I am now ſaying is rather an aſſertion than a demonſtration, yet there is a fact notoriouſly known to all the world, which ſhews that the value of the aſſignats is not regulated by the national affairs of France; for if they were, then the courſe of exchange, and the price of gold and ſilver, would riſe and fall according to the ſucceſs or failure of thoſe perſons who govern the affairs of France; but it is not ſo. The value of the aſſignats hardly varied at all on the 10th of Auguſt, except for a few days; though, the conſtitution being overturned, it was clear that every thing was to do over again, and that therefore the probability of the ſpeedy winding

* The ſame manœuvres have been carried on upon 'Change here in London, where the agents of the treaſury in France have ſold bills on Paris, or bought them at a high price, juſt as it ſuited the purpoſe of keeping up the nominal value of the aſſignat.

up

up of affairs was entirely loſt; and this probability, while it laſted, was certainly one cauſe that gave a real ſolidity to the aſſignat. While the horrid maſſacres of the 2d, 3d, 4th, and 5th of September, were carrying on, the aſſignat was mounting in price; and it aſtoniſhed not a little the merchants on the 'Change at London, that the credit of the paper roſe as the Pruſſian army approached the capital of France, notwithanding it was generally expected that it would ſoon arrive there. This is a plain proof that collateral circumſtances, and not confidence in the ruling ſyſtem of affairs, regulated the value of the aſſignats.

Since the republic, as they call it, has overrun Brabant, and threatened the whole of Europe in a fit of folly and inſolence, their credit ſinks, and the death of their monarch, which they pretended would enſure their proſperity, has ſtill augmented their diſcredit: thus that famous republic, with its claws extended on all ſides, is like a crab, and goes backwards inſtead of advancing.

Such are nearly the reaſons that operate in preſerving a degree of value to the aſſignats, to which their real ſolidity does not entitle them; and theſe reaſons are ſupported with force by the abſolute neceſſity of uſing them, as ſigns of value, there being no other in the whole country.

In what manner, therefore, their real want of ſolidity, added to the great and conſtant increaſe of their quantity, may, in the end, operate, is difficult to gueſs with any degree of preciſion, particularly when theſe cauſes are counteracted by one ſo ſtrong as *abſolute neceſſity*; as they are the only ſigns of value that exiſt over ſuch an extenſive country.

Though from want of precedent of any kind (for the American paper dollar was, in many reſpects, different) it is impoſſible to form a near eſtimate of the time when this paper will have an end; yet it is very certain, that a continual increaſe in the quantity muſt diminiſh the value, and that the diminution muſt go on with an accelerated quickneſs; becauſe the more it loſes, the more will be neceſſary to ſupply the wants of the treaſury,

treaſury, and therefore the creation of paper muſt increaſe in quantity.

They who know little of the matter ſay, that the nominal value ſignifies nothing, or but little, for that two reams of paper muſt be printed off inſtead of one, and then the difficulty is finiſhed. It is indeed true, that there is a certain degree of juſtneſs in this obſervation, but it will not long hold good; becauſe the livre Tournois, though only an ideal value, is the meaſure of the price of many articles, which cannot eaſily be changed; as for inſtance, the price of the four pound loaf of bread, which ought to be 22 ſols at Paris at preſent is but 12 in paper (which is but equal to three-pence Engliſh money). A change cannot be made in ordinary articles progreſſively, and with the ſame rapidity that the paper loſes its value, becauſe the mob taxes all neceſſary articles, and will not allow ſuch augmentations to take place; for every man, as a buyer, conſiders the money he has, and compares it with what he has to buy; nor, indeed, is it poſſible to equalize revenues and prices in ſuch a complex machine as the purchaſes and

ſales

ſales of a great town, like Paris, according to the value of the aſſignat.

When, however, the nature of things is at open war with any contrivance of men, the contrivance muſt, ſooner or later, ſall to the ground.

If the continual importation of gold and ſilver from South America, by increaſing the quantity has diminiſhed its value ſo prodigiouſly, ſince the days of Henry the VIIIth, how much more muſt the increaſe of paper in France, which has but a fictitious value, decreaſe its power of ſerving as money.

The whole quantity of bullion imported into Europe in one year (one with another) has never been eſtimated at more than about 5,000,000 ſterling, and France creates as much currency in twenty-four days. The career down hill muſt be then very rapid indeed.

I write this for the ſatisfaction of the public, and for that reaſon, finding that the different facts and reaſonings about the aſſignats will not lead to any clear conclufion, except the general one of their decreafe in value, I am willing to run the rifk of giving the refult of my own reflexions; fhould time fhew me to be wrong, I hope my countrymen will excufe me.

I think then it is likely that, when the affignat falls to one-third of its value, the order of prices, with regard to buying and felling, will be fo much altered and confufed, that it will occafion an almoft total difcredit of that paper; and I imagine that difcredit muft take place towards the month of May, or June, next; or, at furtheft, by the month of September, fhould our war with them continue.

As foon as the affignats ceafe, then the power of the prefent government, if government it can be called, will ceafe, but not till then; for I do not attempt to deny that fo long as the affignat does fell at a certain price, it is not much matter what that price is, for two reams of paper, inftead of one, will do, and, for the moment, anfwers the fame end;

end; the only difference being, as I ſaid before, that it ſhortens the career.

Thoſe only who have been in France during the Revolution, can tell how powerful an engine the aſſignats have been: had ſome celebrated emigrants taken my advice in the year 1791, *in making war upon the credit of France inſtead of combating her troops*, we ſhould not have had now to arm in England; ſo many brave men would not have bled in the field, nor ſo virtuous a monarch on the ſcaffold.

It has aſtoniſhed me, during theſe three years nearly, (I mean ever ſince the month of June 1790) when the French began to turn their views to Avignon, and lay plans of general conqueſt, that the different nations did not perceive that all their power of doing miſchief lay in the credit of the paper, which they created at will, and expended for the worſt of purpoſes.

I wiſh ſtill to dwell a little more upon this, and ſhall explain myſelf by a ſimilitude which, though very familiar, is very applicable.

Suppofe the wifhing purfe of Fortunatus were to drop into the hands of an individual in London, who had no religion, no morality, nor honour, but who had a fort of wild enthufiaftic defire of dictating to all his neighbours, and difturbing their domeftic peace; and for that purpofe diftributed bribes, paid emiffaries, and ufed every effort that money enables a man to make. Would not all his neighbours foon feel the effects of this, and be rendered very miferable? and not poffeffing fuch a purfe themfelves, muft not they be obliged to fubmit to a thoufand mortifications and inconveniencies? Would not then their beft way be to take from him the fatal purfe, and put it in the fire? after which his reftlefs, mifchievous character would be no longer formidable to them, but muft prey upon himfelf.

It is clear, that as no nation in Europe has 1,000,000 fterling at its command in a year, either for fecret fervices, or at the free difpofition of its fovereign, or his minifters, and as France has twenty, in point of intrigue, corruption, and payment of emiffaries, under whatever defcription they may be, fhe is more

 than

than a match for all the others; if therefore we would gain an eaſy victory over that people, let us undermine their credit*: at the expence of their paper, we ſhall ſave our own blood and treaſure, and, in fact, do them a ſervice; for their power of going on to maſſacre and rob each other cannot be too ſoon put an end to.

There is, I am well aware, an argument that will be uſed againſt what I have ſaid reſpecting the aſſignats, which have now, ſay their advocates, all the eſtates of the emigrants to inſure their payment; and I know this has obtained for them a ſort of credit.

I am not ignorant that there are near fifty thouſand eſtates to ſell; but I am not ignorant either that there are not purchaſers to be found in France for five thouſand of them, nor for two thouſand; ſo that, though theſe lands would no doubt prove a great ſource of revenue, I do not ſee any connection they have with the aſſignats, nor any connection that

* It is evidently not here that the way of undermining their credit is to be diſcuſſed; it is the expediency of the meaſure, not the manner of putting it into execution.

can be created between them. As to people from other nations going into France to buy lands, they may meet with a few dupes, as ignorant youths ſometimes fall in amongſt ſharpers; but a man muſt be very ignorant indeed to purchaſe property in a country, where he muſt have the value ſet upon the produce by a mob, where his life muſt be in danger, and where the ſyſtem of equality tends evidently to an equal diviſion of property.

The fact is, that there are no purchaſers for theſe lands, and that there are not at preſent any methods practiſed for diminiſhing the quantity of aſſignats.

Had France peaceable times, moderate men at the head of affairs, and no foreign war, I ſhould conſider the aſſignats as equal in goodneſs to any paper that is not payable at ſight, or on a certain day; but, ſurrounded as ſhe is with enemies which ſhe has made, torn with internal diſcords, and about to have ſtill more enemies, the ultimate fate of the aſſignats muſt be determined before there can be time to turn about and change the ſyſtem. That the members of the executive council of France, and of the Convention, know their ſtrength to conſiſt in the credit of their aſſignats there is no doubt; and as they know that a war with England will much haſten the ruin of that credit, it is with good reaſon that they wiſh to avoid it.

It would require infinitely longer time than I ſhould think proper to demand of the public, to view the affair of aſſignats ſo completely as it deſerves; and I own frankly I have not the vanity to think myſelf capable of doing the ſubject juſtice; but I think I can maintain againſt whoever wiſhes to combat it, that the credit of the aſſignats is nearly over, and that with them will immediately fall down to nothing the force of the French nation.

But while the aſſignats continue to ſerve the purpoſe, let us ſee how far we in England have a war to fear, and what ſort of exertion the French nation is at preſent capable of making.

First of all we muſt conſider the nature of the effort they have already made, which, having been ſucceſsful, may lead many people

to

to believe, that they are capable of making ſuch another, and finally of conquering their enemies. The laſt campaign was begun too late in the ſeaſon by the combined forces, and with too little warmth; they adopted it partly on compulſion, partly through a generous intention to ſupport the emigrants; and, laſtly, were deceived as to the interior ſtate of the country. The whole weight of the campaign was laid upon the army of the king of Pruſſia, commanded by the duke of Brunſwick, who led the only body of an army ſufficiently great to make any firm reſiſtance.

That this general did not take the precautions neceſſary to ſecure his ſupplies of proviſions is certain; that he committed ſeveral great errors is alſo, if not proved, at leaſt very ſtrongly ſuſpected: but waving theſe diſcuſſions at preſent, ſuppoſe even that Dumourier had all the merit poſſible in his conduct, the retreat of an army half famiſhed and diſeaſed, and in an enemy's country, was not a very great victory, gained by far ſuperior forces. This retreat being once effected, there was not any other body of troops ſufficiently numerous to make head againſt the French army; and the ſucceſs of a few months, on the part of the French, was the inevitable conſequence of the retreat and diſabled condition of the duke's army.

To return once more to the effort made by the French to repel their enemies, let us conſider that the unwiſe manifeſto of the Duke of Brunſwick occaſioned the greateſt effort that it was poſſible for a large city of 700,000 inhabitants, and a populous country, to make. I was in Paris myſelf, and know the feeling which it inſpired. If the Duke's army arrived at Paris, after what had happened on the 10th of Auguſt, nobody could hope for mercy in that city. The Sans Culottes had begun the attack on the palace, and had been ſeconded by the national guards. Now as they forced all the other inhabitants to bear arms, every inhabitant, women and children not excepted, was comprehended in the revolt. The natural conſequence of threatning ſuch a numerous body of people, who had the national treaſury at their command, was, that they would in a fit of deſpair meet their enemies with all the forces they could muſter, and ſo they did. A multitude,

titude, compoſed of all ages and of both ſexes, marched off to repulſe the enemy, who was exactly in ſuch a ſituation as rendered their numbers formidable: at no great diſtance from Paris, ſo that this multitude could eaſily perform the journey, and not having proper ſupplies either of men or proviſions, could he have gained a battle, it is much more than probable that the Duke could never have arrived at Paris. His enemies, on the contrary, were prodigiouſly numerous, actuated by deſpair, and ſupported with every thing they wanted. It was certainly only in hopes of being ſeconded by a party of the people themſelves, that the Duke put himſelf in this ſituation, and he had probably been miſinformed; for though he might have had many friends who otherwiſe would have joined him, his manifeſto rendered it impoſſible for them to act; indeed it took away their inclination; and tho' they might favour the royal cauſe, few people were ready to join againſt their fellow-citizens to put his threats in execution. Notwithſtanding the advantages which the French had of meeting their enemy in a ſick and famiſhed condition, in the heart of their country, in far inferior numbers, it is much

doubted

doubted whether, if a battle had been given, they would not have loſt it; and though Dumourier, certainly with a great ſhare of art and much to his praiſe, contrived to gain time till nothing but a ſhameful retreat was poſſible for his enemies, yet did he not once dare to attack that diſeaſed army in its retreat; inſomuch that all Europe imagined there was a ſort of peace made with the King of Pruſſia. That this was not the caſe has ſince been clearly evident, and Dumourier's enterpriſing ſpirit gives every reaſon to believe, that if then he did not act, it was becauſe he knew he could not act ſucceſsfully.

The overrunning Brabant and Savoy is neither a new ſort of occurrence in war, nor any thing wonderful; nor are ſuch exploits in general of the ſmalleſt advantage. The Turks have beſieged Vienna before now; we have often overrun both France and Spain; the greateſt Emperor Ruſſia ever had was nearly, at one time, driven from his capital, and the great Frederick of Pruſſia, not many years ago, was driven from Berlin; but all this has made no great change in the boundaries of

empires.

empires. We are therefore authorized by hiſtory to conſider ſuch ſucceſſes as of little ſolid importance. But if they are of little importance to well regulated armies, they are of ſtill leſs to numerous armies levied in haſte, as thoſe of France will be in the next campaign. Such armies act with the greateſt advantage upon their own territory, and indeed at a diſtance from home their poſition alone is ſufficient to bring about a defeat.

Invaſions and foreign wars muſt be ſupported by well diſciplined troops, prudent generals, and good precautions taken for ſupplies, but not by great and numerous armies, which it is impoſſible to ſupply at a diſtance.

Some perſons will ſay that Brabant is now become a department of France, but that will not be believed by thoſe who know that men in a country where the language is different, coaleſce with difficulty with the inhabitants; or by thoſe who know how impoſſible it is that the Brabançons can ſo ſoon have adopted the irreligion and levelling principles of their conquerors; principles which it took the volatile French themſelves near four years to attain, with all the incendiary writings, cabals and intrigues, that could be uſed, to bring them to what they are. There are, indeed, people ignorant enough to imagine, that another nation alſo will adopt all this at once; it cannot be; it can but create diſguſt, as actually it does. But it would require too long time, and is too foreign from my ſubject, to ſhew at preſent how amongſt the tricks of French Legiſlators and Commiſſaries, it is one, to make the voice of the minority appear that of the majority, and thereby give every thing the appearance which ſuits their wiſhes and their intereſt.

The ſtate of things then has been, during the laſt campaign, the moſt favourable that was poſſible for armies ſuch as France poſſeſſes; yet is there not a ſingle inſtance when with equal numbers they have gained either a battle or a ſkirmiſh. At Jemappe their number was treble that of the enemy, and though it was their artillery that obtained them the victory, they loſt more than four times as many men as their enemies. The numbers who have periſhed from cold, hunger, and diſeaſe amongſt the French, as well as in ſkirmiſhes, are as ſurpriſingly great, as by the ſtatements to the National Aſſembly they appear ſurpriſingly ſmall; even at Paris the people are not the dupes of that artifice, for thoſe volunteers who have returned have ſometimes told the truth, though it is clear they dare not make it public.

The preſent campaign, whether England had been engaged in it or not, muſt be very different from the laſt. The King of Pruſſia and the whole Empire (before it was but the Emperor, as King of Hungary and Bohemia) fight for their own political exiſtence, and therefore will fight well; from being auxiliaries they are become principals; inſtead of beginning in the month of Auguſt they are now nearly ready to begin, and they will not a ſecond time be deceived with regard to the ſtate of the country, neither is it likely that they will publiſh manifeſtos of the ſame nature.

The finances of France are prodigiouſly more exhauſted ſince that period, and the remains of the unfortunate Houſe of Bourbon,

 the

the Dauphin excepted, who is too young to reign, and is besides a prisoner, are all with the confederate armies; and will enter France to claim what a great part of the nation still think their right, the throne of their ancestors.

As to discipline, it will not be much meliorated in the French armies since last year, because these soldiers of liberty quit their post when they chuse, and the new armies will be formed this spring chiefly from raw recruits.

Such are the prospects of France with respect to her German enemies; on the side of Savoy also there will certainly be a diversion sufficient to divide her forces, occupy a part of her attention, and exhaust her finances. Let us now come to the possible exertions of France against England and Holland.

The manning and commanding of a navy is a very different thing from sending out a land army like Dumourier's, for it depends not upon multitudes and numbers, and least

of

of all upon that impetuous effort which acts only for a few weeks.

If with all the millions wasted, clothing for 400,000 men could never be had, because there is neither industry nor arrangement in the country, clothing which could not cost one million sterling, how are the ships of a squadron to be furnished with what is necessary?

For the marine of France, which never was equal to ours, there were about 1200 officers necessary, and in last August there were not 200 at all the different ports. From the brave Albert de Rioms, down to the midshipman, almost every officer was disgusted with that system of equality, which by a sort of paradox, not easily to be understood, gave the crew the right of commanding, and therefore imposed upon the officers a necessity to obey.

By land, sudden exertions may be made, and every man counts for a soldier, but it is not so by sea; the preparations are tedious, require care, and are after all limited in their extent.

extent. It is not here that the Marſeillois and the aſſaſſins from the garrets in the ſuburbs of Paris, led on by valet de chambres and girls, will defend their country againſt our brave Engliſh ſeamen, and experienced captains.

I know, however, that the French will have men enough to man their navy, and more than they have ſhips to man, nor will theſe be landſmen; having now little or no trade, they will eaſily find ſeamen, and here it ſhould be obſerved, that the poverty and miſery of the country ſerves in ſome meaſure to give it ſtrength, for all thoſe men who are without work to do, and bread to eat, are ready to fly to its defence.

The French marine wants officers, and it will be impoſſible for them to equip, in a complete manner, above one half of their ſhips. They want alſo diſcipline; for it is no exaggeration of the matter to ſay, that the men will not obey their officers; and this is ſo true, that many officers who are well enough diſpoſed to defend their country, have left the ſervice, merely becauſe they know that the

men

men only obey whilſt it is their good pleaſure ſo to do, but that when they are diſpleaſed, they immediately put their captain in irons.

To all this it is to be added, that France will require ſupplies of corn and other proviſions by ſea, next ſummer, to prevent a famine, which a war with England will render it impoſſible for them to obtain. This may appear to be an aſſertion made upon the faith of thoſe rumours of famine already ſpread, but it is not ſo.

By all ſtatements, and amongſt others thoſe of Mr. Necker, France exported of grain of all ſorts, one year with another, the value of 10 millions Tournois, which is not enough to ſupply the inhabitants of that country one fortnight. The quantity of grain exported on an average from any country, is the meaſure of the ſurplus produced above what is conſumed, which this ſtatement proves to be very little.

Ever ſince the revolution began, France has been in want of grain, and obliged to have ſupplies, becauſe the circulation in the interior, from one town to another, has been greatly interrupted, and becaufe agriculture has been in fome degree neglected.

The circulation continues to be interrupted, which caufe alone is fufficient to produce a partial famine; and laft year the harveft was neglected more than ever: add to this, that the men in arms confume much more than men at home. From all thefe caufes a famine is certain, if no fupplies come in from other countries. It is, moreover, certain, that neither laft year, nor the year before, were fo plentiful as the year 1790, and even then there was not enough for the home confumption, without foreign aid.

From the paper read by Mr. Kerfaint to the Convention, on a war with England, as well as from citizen Briffot's report, it would appear that their views extend to South America and our territories in the Eaft and Weft Indies: fuch propofitions, in the prefent circumftances of France, are perfectly contemptible; and it is only in the Convention, or the Jacobin club, that the ignorance of men is great enough to liften to them without hiffing the reader from his place.

In the prefent war, England may likewife reckon much upon the ignorance of all thofe who are employed in the marine and war departments; as on purpofe to have, what they called, ftaunch patriots, they, laft year, turned out almoft all the clerks and fecretaries employed, and put in Jacobins who know nothing of the nature of thefe affairs. This will appear to be a fact of no fmall importance to thofe who know, that in great and complicated affairs, a knowledge of the routine in which bufinefs has been ufed to go, is very neceffary.

We may likewife, in this war, count upon that fpirit of contradiction which fruftrates exertion in every country where there are people of different parties; and we may be affured, that the town council of Breft, and the other fea ports, will not always be of the fame opinion as the minifter of the marine, who will therefore be croffed in many of his operations, as he has always been in every armament for St. Domingo.

The injury that their privateers may do to our trade is the chief thing we have to fear;

 but

but even that is more imaginary than real; for unleſs they can cope with us, or nearly ſo, in ſhips of the line, the depredations by privateers will not be of much importance.

The queſtion of war or peace, it was not my buſineſs to diſcuſs: I know not the ſecret negociations, nor the conceſſions which the French might make; but were I to have given my private opinion, it would have been, that unleſs France abandoned, in the moſt ſolemn and complete manner, all idea of ſpreading her dominion, or extending her ſyſtem of equality into other nations, it would be beſt for us to join in bringing her to reaſon. Self-preſervation ſeems to be no leſs the law of political bodies than of individuals; and it is certain, that ſhould France ſucceed in her projects on the Continent, England muſt in the end ſubmit. I do not, indeed, imagine France would ſucceed though England ſhould remain neuter; but the poſſibility of her doing ſo would, in that caſe, be greater, and for that reaſon we ought, in prudence, to bear our part in putting an end to her career.

War is certainly to be avoided, if with honour and ſafety it can. The bleſſings of peace are ineſtimable, and certainly more ſo at this time than almoſt at any other; but without France abandons her ſyſtem of univerſal liberty, as ſhe calls it, our peace could have been of no long continuance; nor can the leaſt faith be given to her promiſes, becauſe the avowed ſyſtem of the levellers is, that might creates right; and whatever they have the power and will to do, they think may lawfully be done.

It ſeems very clear that from a war with France we have, at preſent, very little to fear; we may reſt aſſured that it will be a ſhort one; and I am convinced, that if we act in concert with the powers on the Continent, and if, inſtead of a bloody manifeſto like the duke of Brunſwick's, a wiſe and mild one ſhall precede the army that is to enter France, nothing will be more acceptable to the great bulk of the French nation, than to ſee order re-eſtabliſhed, in any manner that may form ſomething like a reaſonable government.

The French have, both publicly and privately, declared that they will ſend one hundred thouſand men to invade this country: there is little doubt but they will attempt it, if it was for no other purpoſe but to rid their country of part of its unfortunate and wretched inhabitants: whether they go to the bottom of the ſea in their attempt to come over, or are deſtroyed at the mouth of our cannon, would be of no conſequence to the National Convention, as from the effect of their proceedings, a famine muſt, in a ſhort time, take them off were they to ſtay in their own country.

By their equality they have deſtroyed nobility and gentry; of courſe, all artizans in every branch of buſineſs tending to luxury, are out of employ, and are obliged to live as a prey upon the public. For inſtance: What would become of the tradeſmen in London, and the public at large, were the nobility and gentry to be chaſed out of the country? This muſt be better felt than it can be deſcribed, as it is well known to every individual, that all arts, ſciences, and trade, have flouriſhed, and ſtill proſper, by the wants of the great and opulent of this kingdom.

There

There are many perſons in the world to whom vengeance is ſweet; and perhaps it is unfortunately but too true, that the violent proceedings of the French make them very proper objects of anger. But revenge ought never to be the ruling paſſion of man in any caſe, and leaſt of all ought it to be ever directed againſt a multitude, in which great numbers muſt be innocent, others ignorant, and only a few guilty.

Though I am, and never have concealed it, even when I ran ſome perſonal riſk, a great enemy to the French democrats: though I know their villainy, and the unfairneſs of their way of reaſoning, I am far from thinking the majority of the nation guilty; on the contrary in Paris, where the guilt is certainly the greateſt, I am certain that nine out of ten deſerve cenſure, only for not having had courage enough to act when it was neceſſary.

Men, individually brave, do not always act in civil broils as if they were ſo; becauſe, as no ſingle exertion can produce any good effect, they only act when they have confidence in others who will act with them. Now, very

unfor-

unfortunately for the inhabitants of Paris, as they had been accuſtomed to a ſort of implicit obedience in affairs of government, and were obliged all at once to become governors, ignorant at the ſame time of the true baſis of liberty, and its firſt principles, which. it is too late for men to learn on a ſudden at years of maturity, there could be no unity nor mutual confidence among them: nor could even the great neceſſity of the caſe unite the inhabitants of a city, formerly drowned in luxury and pleaſure; and, ever ſince its revolt, the ſport of intrigue.

Before the Revolution, France was infinitely too much corrupted for its inhabitants to take advantage of the feeble ſtate of its Monarch, ſo as to eſtabliſh liberty; which to men of purer manners and of a leſs volatile character, would, at one time, have been not very difficult. At preſent it is only by wading through oceans of blood, and letting adverſity and time teach wiſdom to them, that they can ever gain this end. Nay, it is much more probable that they will fall under the hand of ſome deſpot before they can accompliſh their deſign; for at preſent, governed as they are

by

by the lower order of people, who are the dupes and agents of the moſt deſigning amongſt themſelves, Revolution muſt follow Revolution, until poverty, and equality in miſery, will put an end to the conteſt; for as long as they who take the lead can have the means of enriching themſelves, others, who want to be rich alſo, will overturn them and take their place, as it has happened already.

It is unlucky that in England any language, truly deſcriptive of theſe proceedings, and of the perſons who govern Paris, is diſgraceful, and ſeems like the language of anger and prejudice. Facts ſeem exaggerations; and ſuch epithets as ſuit the caſe, can only, with propriety, be uſed at Billingſgate. I ſhall not therefore attempt to deſcribe the manner in which Paris governs France, but ſhall beg leave literally to tranſlate language which I myſelf have heard employed by the people in the gallery of the National Aſſembly to its members; and language which had the immediate effect of making the Aſſembly obey. I never was lucky enough to be preſent at a very tumultuous debate. This is a ſpecimen of what paſſed on every ordinary day, when any queſtion that intereſted the court, or his late majeſty, was diſcuſſed*.

Upon a queſtion ſeeming to go in favour of the king, the galleries roſe, and ſaid, with violent geſtures and menaces, " Go home, " you raſcals; you men hired at eighteen " ſhillings a day; you don't deſerve them. " Shame, ſhame, you betray us; we are " your maſters; you are but deputies paid; " you have ſold us to the civil liſt, you " anointed curs; but we know how to be " revenged upon raſcals like you, who were " eat up with poverty and lice till we took " you into pay, and you dare to betray the " nation, you dogs!"

I can only ſay, that the French expreſſions were yet ſtronger than thoſe I give. This happened in an evening ſitting. I was in what is called " The Suppleant's Gallery,"

* The queſtion was concerning the terrace in the garden of the Thuilleries, which garden being ſhut, they wanted to make public, and by means of that queſtion to animate the people againſt the king; in which they ſucceeded very rapidly, and very completely.

which

which had but few people in it, though the public galleries were very full.

The effect of these threats was instantaneous; and on counting the voices the third time, for the question had been divided, it was found to be determined against the king, against justice, and against common sense. Such was, and still continues to be, the manner in which the violent party triumphs over the majority, upon all occasions, in which it is thought to be worth while. Yet the nation in which laws are so passed, pretends to be free, and to present an example worthy the imitation of all the world. It is not from men governed in this manner that England has any thing to fear; and it is surprising that there should be men in England so lost to every sense of shame as to praise the French government; and what adds considerably to the disgrace of some such persons is, that they know, perfectly well, that what I now have said about the galleries is strictly true.

It is notoriously known to all the world, that on the 10th of August the Assembly passed decrees at the request of every blackguard who appeared at the bar, without so much as enquiring their names, in many cafes; and all the decrees paffed unanimoufly for feveral days.

Thus a ragged fellow, without coat or hat, and covered with blood, appeared in the name of the nation, and demanded the dethroning of the king; others demanded a republic, and a convention, liberty and equality; and, fince that time, it is by the fame means that they have brought their unhappy monarch to the block; loading him, during his confinement, with abufe, from which, if his former quality of king, if even his virtues and love of his people could not exempt him, he fhould at leaft have been fhielded by his misfortunes.

The French nation is in a ftate of madnefs and rage, dangerous to thofe who, without precaution, approach too near, as individual madmen are; but to thofe who, taking the proper meafures, attack them where they are leaft able to refift, the danger can be but fmall, and even then muft be but of fhort duration. Without plan, without order, and without induftry, what nation can long be formidable? and that the French have any one of thefe great requifites to all fuccefs, I defy their moft firm friends and ſtrongeſt advocates to prove; and till they can do ſo, I muſt perſiſt in thinking my concluſions no leſs juſt and incontrovertible, than I truſt they will prove ſalutary to the nation, in preventing all unreaſonable apprehenſion or deſpondency.

Since writing my *General View of the Actual Force and Reſources of France*, I have thought of a method of calculating the rate, at which the aſſignats will probably decreaſe in value from their *increaſe in quantity*.

The

The TABLE is ſubjoined, and the grounds upon which it is calculated are as follows:

	Sterl.
1. That the whole creation of aſſignats is actually equal to - -	112,000,000
2. That this quantity of paper only repreſents a ſum in ſpecie, of gold or ſilver, equal to - - -	50,000,000
3. That the expence of each month in France amount to a ſum, in ſpecie, equal to - - -	4,000,000
4. That the wealth of the individuals of the nation is diminiſhing, every month, at the rate of - - -	1,000,000

If theſe data are right, then the diminution of the value of the aſſignats, during the firſt month, will be 112,000,000 ÷ 50,000,000 = 2,250,000 × 4 = 8,900,000, which laſt ſum is neceſſary for this month. Now this is to be added to 112,000,000 for the beginning of next month, which as the whole property diminiſhes, is to be divided by 49, and thus the operation is to be repeated for every future month.

TABLE ſhewing the monthly Increaſe in Quantity, and Diminution in Value, of the French Aſſignats, calculated after the foregoing Data, which, though certainly not Exact, are not very far from it.

Months from this Time 1793.	Total Quantity of Aſſignats created.	Real Value repreſented by the Aſſignats.	Value of Paper which is equal to 1 Million in Specie.	Monthly Sum in Specie.	Sum Neceſſary for Expences per Month.	Rate of Exchange as it ought to be.
February	112,000,000	50,000,000	2,250,000	4	8,900,000	13,2
March	120,900,000	49,000,000	2,467,000	4	9,868,000	12,2
April	130,768,000	48,000,000	2,724,000	4	10,896,000	11,0
May	141,164,000	47,000,000	3,003,000	4	12,012,000	9,99
June	153,492,000	46,000,000	3,329,000	4	13,316,000	9,01
July	166,288,000	45,000,000	3,699,000	4	14,796,000	8,11
Auguſt	181,768,000	44,000,000	4,120,000	4	16,480,000	7,28
September	197,164,000	43,000,000	4,599,000	4	18,396,000	6,52
October	216,748,000	42,000,000	5,146,000	4	20,584,000	5,82
November	236,844,000	41,000,000	5,774,000	4	23,096,000	5,19
December	259,826,000	40,000,000	6,496,000	4	25,982,000	4,61
Janua. 1794	285,138,000	39,000,000	7,328,000	4	29,312,000	4,09
February	315,310,000	38,000,000	8,293,000	4	53,172,000	3,61
March	348,962,000	37,000,000	9,413,000	4	37,652,000	3,18
April	385,846,000	36,000,000	10,721,000	4	42,884,000	2,79
May	428,854,000	35,000,000	12,252,000	4	49,008,000	2,44
June	477,070,000	34,000,000	14,054,000	4	56,216,000	2,13
July	534,802,000	33,000,000	16,183,000	4	64,732,000	1,85
Auguſt	598,662,000	32,000,000	18,715,000	4	74,860,000	1,60
September	673,586,000	31,000,000	21,731,000	4	86,924,000	1,38
October	760,586,000	30,000,000	25,352,000	4	100,408,000	1,20
November	860,994,000	29,000,000	29,689,000	4	118,756,000	1,01
December	970,750,000	28,000,000	34,990,000	4	1[illegible],960,000	0,83

It

It is evident, that as my data are not very exact, ſo neither can be my reſults: that as numbers of collateral cauſes are continually operating, which are totally incalculable, I ſhall never find my table verified by experience with any degree of nearneſs; but I do conſider it as a matter both of curious and important inquiry, to calculate how quickly the aſſignat has a tendency to ſink in value from its own nature only. I have already obſerved, that as circumſtances may happen to retard or haſten this depreciation, we can only count upon that diſcredit which the nature of things attaches to its exiſtence: thus the life of man, though eſtimated at 70 years, is liable to be ſhortened or lengthened: but he who calculates upon the nature and ſtrength of man in general, will be right in his concluſions *in general*, though not in particular caſes.

Such is the brilliant career which the conſtant augmentation of the quantity of aſſignats prepares for that paper, which has, during three years, ſupported French vanity, French anarchy, and French infamy. The vanity will have a fall with the aſſignats, the anarchy will outlive them a long time, but the infamy will be eternal.

By Authority

This Day is publiſhed, in One Volume, Royal Quarto,

Conſiſting of Six Hundred Pages of cloſe Letter Preſs, Pr. 1l. 11s. 6d. in Bds.

Illuſtrated with Seventeen Maps, Charts, Views, and other Embelliſhments, drawn on the Spot, by Captains HUNTER and BRADLEY, and Lieut. DAWES,

AN HISTORICAL JOURNAL OF THE TRANSACTIONS AT PORT JACKSON AND NORFOLK ISLAND,

With the Diſcoveries which have been made in NEW SOUTH WALES, and in the Southern Ocean, ſince the Publication of PHILLIP's VOYAGE, compiled from the Official Papers;

Including the Journals of Governors PHILLIP and KING, and of Lieut. BALL; and the Voyages from the firſt Sailing of the Sirius in 1787, to the Return of that Ship's Company to England in 1792.

By JOHN HUNTER, Eſq;

POST CAPTAIN IN HIS MAJESTY'S NAVY.

LONDON: Printed for JOHN STOCKDALE, Piccadilly.

A Liſt of the PLATES in the above WORK.

1. A Portrait of Captain Hunter,
2. Vignette on the Title Page of a Native Woman and Child in Diſtreſs,
3. A large Map of New South Wales, ſhewing the River Hawkeſbury and every Part of that Country hitherto explored, by Lieut. Dawes.
4. A large Chart of Botany-Bay, Port Jackſon, and Broken Bay, with the intermediate Coaſt and Soundings, ſurveyed by Capt. Hunter.
5. The Southern Hemiſphere, ſhewing the Track of the Syrius,
6. A new Plan of Norfolk-Iſland, by Captain Bradley,
7. Track of the Waakſamheyd Tranſport, } By Capt. Hunter.
8. A View of the Settlement on Sydney Cove, Port Jackſon, } By Capt. Hunter.
9. A View of the Settlement at Roſe-Hill, } By Capt. Hunter.
10. Canoes of the Admiralty Iſlands, } By Capt. Hunter.
11. A Man of Lord Howe's Groupe, } By Capt. Hunter.
12. Canoes of the Duke of York's Iſland, } By Capt. Hunter.
13. A Man of the Duke of York's-Iſland } By Capt. Hunter.
14. A Family of New South Wales, by Governor King,
15. Non-Deſcript Shells, of New South Wales, Plate I.
16. Ditto - - - - - - - Plate II.
17. Ditto - - - - - - - Plate III.

*** *A few Copies of the above Work may be had printed on a Superfine, Wove Royal, Price 2l. 2s. in Boards.*

SPLENDID EDITION OF GAY'S FABLES.

This Day is publiſhed,

IN TWO VOLUMES,

ELEGANTLY PRINTED ON A SUPERFINE, WOVE, ELEPHANT OCTAVO, (11 INCHES by 7,)

And embelliſhed with Seventy Copper Plates,

Engraved by MR. HALL, GRAINGER, AUDINET, BLAKE, MAZELL, LOVEGROVE, WILSON, SKELTON, and COOKE.

Price One Pound Eleven Shillings and Six-pence in Boards,

FABLES,

By *JOHN GAY.*

TO WHICH IS PREFIXED A LIFE OF THE AUTHOR.

LONDON: PRINTED FOR JOHN STOCKDALE, PICCADILLY.

This Work has been carefully hot-preſſed, and will be delivered in Boards, with Silver Paper betwixt each Plate and the Letter Preſs, to prevent the one from injuring the Beauty of the other.

Piccadilly, Feb. 16, 1793.

TRAVELS

THROUGH

SICILY AND CALABRIA,

IN THE YEAR 1791,

WITH A POSTSCRIPT,

Containing ſome Account of the Ceremonies of the laſt Holy Week at Rome, and of a ſhort Excurſion to Tivoli.

BY THE REV. BRIAN HILL, A.M.

Late of QUEEN'S COLLEGE, OXFORD, and CHAPLAIN to the EARL of LEVEN and MELVILL.

In One Volume Royal Octavo with a Map, Price 7s. 6d.

www.ingramcontent.com/pod-product-compliance
Lightning Source LLC
Chambersburg PA
CBHW031756090426
42739CB00008B/1029

* 9 7 8 3 3 3 7 7 8 0 0 3 6 *